BIPOLAR DISORDERS

MENTAL ILLNESSES AND DISORDERS

MENTAL ILLNESSES AND DISORDERS
Awareness and Understanding

BIPOLAR
DISORDERS

H.W. Poole

SERIES CONSULTANT
ANNE S. WALTERS, PhD
Chief Psychologist, Emma Pendleton Bradley Hospital
Clinical Associate Professor, Alpert Medical School/Brown University

MASON CREST

Mason Crest
450 Parkway Drive, Suite D
Broomall, PA 19008
www.masoncrest.com

MTM Publishing, Inc.
435 West 23rd Street, #8C
New York, NY 10011
www.mtmpublishing.com

President: Valerie Tomaselli
Vice President, Book Development: Hilary Poole
Designer: Annemarie Redmond
Copyeditor: Peter Jaskowiak
Editorial Assistant: Andrea St. Aubin

Series ISBN: 978-1-4222-3364-1
ISBN: 978-1-4222-3369-6
Ebook ISBN: 978-1-4222-8570-1

Library of Congress Cataloging-in-Publication Data
Poole, Hilary W., author.
  Bipolar disorder / by H.W. Poole.
      pages cm. — (Mental illnesses and disorders: awareness and understanding)
  Includes bibliographical references and index.
  ISBN 978-1-4222-3369-6 (hardback) — ISBN 978-1-4222-3364-1 (series) —
ISBN 978-1-4222-8570-1 (ebook)
1. Manic-depressive illness—Juvenile literature. I. Title.
  RC516.P64 2016
  616.89'5—dc23
                                    2015006835

Printed and bound in the United States of America.

First printing
9 8 7 6 5 4 3 2 1

TABLE OF CONTENTS

Key Icons to Look for:

Words to Understand: These words with their easy-to-understand definitions will increase the reader's understanding of the text, while building vocabulary skills.

Sidebars: This boxed material within the main text allows readers to build knowledge, gain insights, explore possibilities, and broaden their perspectives by weaving together additional information to provide realistic and holistic perspectives.

Research Projects: Readers are pointed toward areas of further inquiry connected to each chapter. Suggestions are provided for projects that encourage deeper research and analysis.

Text-Dependent Questions: These questions send the reader back to the text for more careful attention to the evidence presented there.

Series Glossary of Key Terms: This back-of-the-book glossary contains terminology used throughout the series. Words found here increase the reader's ability to read and comprehend higher-level books and articles in this field.

People who cope with mental illnesses and disorders deserve our empathy and respect.

Introduction to the Series

According to the National Institute of Mental Health, in 2012 there were an estimated 45 million people in the United States suffering from mental illness, or 19 percent of all US adults. A separate 2011 study found that among children, almost one in five suffer from some form of mental illness or disorder. The nature and level of impairment varies widely. For example, children and adults with anxiety disorders may struggle with a range of symptoms, from a constant state of worry about both real and imagined events to a complete inability to leave the house. Children or adults with schizophrenia might experience periods when the illness is well controlled by medication and therapies, but there may also be times when they must spend time in a hospital for their own safety and the safety of others. For every person with mental illness who makes the news, there are many more who do not, and these are the people that we must learn more about and help to feel accepted, and even welcomed, in this world of diversity.

It is not easy to have a mental illness in this country. Access to mental health services remains a significant issue. Many states and some private insurers have "opted out" of providing sufficient coverage for mental health treatment. This translates to limits on the amount of sessions or frequency of treatment, inadequate rates for providers, and other problems that make it difficult for people to get the care they need.

Meanwhile, stigma about mental illness remains widespread. There are still whispers about "bad parenting," or "the other side of the tracks." The whisperers imply that mental illness is something you bring upon yourself, or something that someone does to you. Obviously, mental illness can be exacerbated by an adverse event such as trauma or parental instability. But there is just as much truth to the biological bases of mental illness. No one is made schizophrenic by ineffective parenting, for example, or by engaging in "wild" behavior as an adolescent. Mental illness is a complex interplay of genes, biology, and the environment, much like many physical illnesses.

People with mental illness are brave soldiers, really. They fight their illness every day, in all of the settings of their lives. When people with an anxiety disorder graduate from college, you know that they worked very hard to get there—harder, perhaps, than those who did not struggle with a psychiatric issue. They got up every day with a pit in their stomach about facing the world, and they worried about their finals more than their classmates. When they had to give a presentation in class, they thought their world was going to end and that they would faint, or worse, in front of everyone. But they fought back, and they kept going. Every day. That's bravery, and that is to be respected and congratulated.

These books were written to help young people get the facts about mental illness. Facts go a long way to dispel stigma. Knowing the facts gives students the opportunity to help others to know and understand. If your student lives with someone with mental illness, these books can help students know a bit more about what to expect. If they are concerned about someone, or even about themselves, these books are meant to provide some answers and a place to start.

The topics covered in this series are those that seem most relevant for middle schoolers—disorders that they are most likely to come into contact with or to be curious about. Schizophrenia is a rare illness, but it is an illness with many misconceptions and inaccurate portrayals in media. Anxiety and depressive disorders, on the other hand, are quite common. Most of our youth have likely had personal experience of anxiety or depression, or knowledge of someone who struggles with these symptoms.

As a teacher or a librarian, thank you for taking part in dispelling myths and bringing facts to your children and students. Thank you for caring about the brave soldiers who live and work with mental illness. These reference books are for all of them, and also for those of us who have the good fortune to work with and know them.

—Anne S. Walters, PhD
Chief Psychologist, Emma Pendleton Bradley Hospital
Clinical Professor, Alpert Medical School/Brown University

CHAPTER ONE

EMOTIONAL EXTREMES

Words to Understand

bipolar: involving two, opposite ends.

context: the larger situation in which something happens.

depression: a feeling of hopelessness and lack of energy.

euphoria: a feeling of extreme, even overwhelming, happiness.

excessive: too much of something.

grandiosity: a person's belief that he or she is greater or more important than everyone else.

manic: a high level of excitement or energy.

We all have days when we feel good and days when we don't. Every once in a while, something terrible happens, and then we might not feel good for quite a while. But little by little, we usually do start to feel better.

It's like we're walking along a road. The road might slope up or dip down. The scenery might be pretty or ugly. But the changes are gradual. The road we are on today looks pretty much the same as it did yesterday.

For people with **bipolar** disorders, things are more difficult. Life can feel less like a road and more like a rollercoaster.

What Is Bipolar Disorder?

Having strong emotions is not the same as having a bipolar disorder. Some people are naturally emotional. It's not a disorder, it's just who they are.

People with bipolar disorder alternate between feeling *very* "up" and *very* "down," and these extreme feelings are difficult for them to manage. That is, they tend to feel like they are not really in control—their moods are in control instead. Doctors call these extremes **manic** and **depressive**. Later, we will talk about what these states feel and look like. But first, it's important to understand that **context** is very important.

Let's say you are hanging out with your best friend, and he says something funny. You laugh, and then your friend laughs at you laughing, and then you laugh more because your friend is laughing so hard. There's no problem here. It's just you and your buddy being silly.

Or let's think about the reverse. For example, if someone you love dies. You may not want to laugh, or eat, or even get out of bed for a while. You might feel like you'll never

Opposite: Actual roller coasters can be fun, but when your emotions feel like a roller coaster, it can be exhausting.

People with bipolar disorder feel very "up" or very "down," but without any clear reason why.

be happy again. That's understandable: you're grieving. It's natural to feel terrible for a time.

People with bipolar disorder have the extreme emotions we just described, but *without* the context. They feel very "up" or very "down" but with no clear reason why. These emotions interfere with the things they do every day—attending school or work, having friends, and so on. This is why bipolar disorders are a problem. It's not that emotions are bad. It's that the emotions are so strong that people can't live the lives they want to live.

Depressive Episodes

We've all felt depressed at one time or another. Everything looks a bit gray and uninteresting. We don't have the energy for things we normally like. These are all normal ways to feel sometimes.

But if someone feels that way constantly and for a long time, it could be what doctors call a depressive episode. Symptoms of depression usually include:

- sadness
- low energy
- feeling worthless
- trouble concentrating
- pains, like stomachaches and headaches, with no obvious cause
- eating a lot or not much at all
- sleeping a lot or not much at all
- having thoughts of self-harm
- feeling **excessive** guilt

There is a type of mood disorder called depression, which involves having these feelings most or all of the time. But someone with a bipolar disorder will switch between this type of low mood and another, called mania.

ABOUT CYCLING

Going from a depressed state to a manic one and back again is called cycling. Adults with bipolar disorder can stay in one state for days, weeks, or even months. But kids with bipolar disorder sometimes go from one state to the other more quickly. This is called rapid cycling. Some kids with bipolar disorder have more than one extreme mood per day.

Manic Episodes

In certain ways, a manic episode is the opposite of depression: the person has a *lot* of energy. Someone in a manic episode will not sleep much but won't seem tired. She will talk faster than normal. She may have trouble staying focused on one subject. This last experience is sometimes called a "flight of ideas" because so many thoughts are "flying" through the person's head at the same time. She might have a lot of

For kids with bipolar disorder, a manic episode might involve a lot of tantrums and acting out.

projects going at once, or she might be thinking about starting lots of activities.

However, manic episodes are not *exactly* the opposite of depression. After all, the opposite of "depressed" should be "happy." And sometimes people with bipolar disorder do experience a state of **euphoria**. But often, they don't actually feel very happy when in a manic state.

In fact, a manic episode can make someone extremely irritable. You can imagine why that might be—it must be very frustrating to feel like you can't sit still, rest, or relax, even if you want to. It can be pretty scary to feel like you can't control your own emotions or behavior. This is especially true with kids. Kids in a manic episode tend to be very grouchy, not euphoric. They get very angry or upset easily. They also tend to have tantrums or "act out" a lot.

Another problem with mania is that people tend to do risky things. Someone in a manic episode might go shopping, for example, and spend huge amounts of money she doesn't

DID YOU KNOW?

According to the National Institute of Mental Health, about 2.6 percent of the US population has a bipolar disorder. That's about 5.6 million people.

MIXED EPISODES

It sounds like it should be obvious whether someone with bipolar disorder is depressed or manic. And frequently that's true: it is obvious. But sometimes people have what are called mixed episodes, when they show symptoms of both depression and mania at the same time. A person might be silly or giddy but still feel worthless and sad on the inside.

have. She doesn't think about the consequences because her mania is telling her that she can do whatever she wants. People in a manic state tend to feel that they are better than others, or that rules don't apply to them. Doctors call this **grandiosity**.

One specific type of manic episode is called hypomania. The prefix *hypo-* means "under." Hypomania is a less severe version of mania. People in this state tend to feel very "up" and energetic, but they are more in control than people in

Winston Churchill was prime minister of Great Britain from 1940 to 1945 and 1951 to 1955. A friend described him as always "at the top of the wheel of confidence or at the bottom of an intense depression." This has led historians to suspect Churchill may have had bipolar disorder.

fully manic episodes. A lot of the behaviors are the same, but hypomanic episodes don't cause as many problems in daily life as manic episodes do.

Types of Bipolar Disorders

There are four main types of bipolar disorders. These types are defined by the type of episodes a person has.

Bipolar I. With this type, there has been at least one manic episode, and this episode has to have lasted at least seven days.

Bipolar II. With this second type, there has been at least one period of depression and one hypomanic episode.

Cyclothymia. A person with cyclothymia will have had two years of alternating manic and depressive symptoms that are not as severe as the above types. The prefix *cyclo-* refers to the cycling of moods.

Bipolar disorder not otherwise specified. A person with this type has some symptoms, but not enough to qualify as one of the above types.

Text-Dependent Questions

1. What are some symptoms of a depressive episode?
2. What are some symptoms of a manic episode?
3. How is hypomania different from mania?
4. What is different about manic episodes in kids as opposed to adults?

Research Project

The painter Edvard Munch wrote, "My fear of life is necessary to me, as is my illness." The notable figures listed below all probably suffered from some form of mood disorder, such as bipolar disorder or depression. Choose one and learn more about his or her work. How might their disorders have hurt their work? How might they have helped?

- Winston Churchill
- Ernest Hemingway
- Edvard Munch
- Florence Nightingale
- Jackson Pollack
- Vincent Van Gogh
- Virginia Woolf

CHAPTER TWO

THE BRAIN AND BIPOLAR DISORDER

Words to Understand

neuron: a specialized nerve cell.

neurotransmitter: chemical in the brain that carries messages from neuron to neuron.

onset: the beginning of something; pronounced like "on" and "set."

receptor: part of a nerve cell that "catches" neurotransmitters.

synapse: a tiny gap between two nerve cells.

Some people believe that "bipolar" is just a fancy term for being "moody." But this is a myth. Having bipolar disorder does not mean that you switch from happy to sad instantly. Manic and depressive episodes can each last for days or weeks.

The last chapter talked about what bipolar disorders look and feel like. Now let's talk about what is happening in the brain of someone with the disorder.

Brain Messages

Your brain is basically a three-pound communications center. Information comes in from your senses: what you see, hear, smell, touch, and so on. The brain interprets these messages and sends responses back to the body. Billions of messages are sent and received by your brain in a single day. And this all happens so quickly that you don't even notice.

The messages are carried through your brain along a network of cells called **neurons**. Neurons have space between

THE BRAIN'S NEEDS

MRI Head Scan   AS
Ex: 29942
Se: 8
In: 4

R   R

1   1
2   0
8   0

All those neurons sending all those messages require a lot of energy. In fact, about a fifth of your blood is pumped from your heart to your brain. The brain also uses about a fifth of all the oxygen you breathe.

them; these spaces are called **synapses**. So how do neurons pass messages to each other if they can't touch? Messages are sent using special chemicals, called **neurotransmitters**.

Imagine that you are playing baseball. You are in center field, and you need to send a message to the catcher. You write a note, attach it to the ball, and throw the ball to home plate. Your message travels between you and the catcher, but you never touch the catcher or speak to him directly. How? Because the message was attached to the ball. Neurons in your brain work roughly the same way. A neuron "fires," or releases a neurotransmitter, to carry its message across the synapse. Once it is released, the neuron looks for the right **receptor**—in the baseball example, that would be the catcher's glove.

Once the message is delivered, the receptor doesn't need the neurotransmitter any more. So the receptor releases the neurotransmitter back into the synapse. This would be like the catcher throwing the ball back onto the field.

The Bipolar Brain

Specific parts of your brain are in charge of managing your moods. Of course, whether you are happy or sad is partly a reaction to what is going on around you. But your feelings are also influenced by the neurons in these particular parts of the brain. And a lot can go wrong. In fact, we are not always sure exactly what is happening. But scientists do have theories.

Going back to our baseball example, imagine that you want to send a *billion* messages to the catcher. You'd need a lot of baseballs! What if you didn't have as many as you needed? Or let's say you have enough baseballs at first. But after the catcher receives the message, he tosses them into the crowd instead of back to the center fielder? It won't be long before you run low.

Or what if the opposite happens? What if the center fielder is replaced by a pitching machine, and it fires baseballs at the catcher so quickly that he can't possibly catch them all?

These examples describe what is probably happening in the brains of people with bipolar disorder. During a depressive episode, their brains may not be producing enough neurotransmitters. Or it is possible that the neurotransmitters are simply not working well.

Manic episodes probably work in the opposite way. There may be too many neurotransmitters for the receptors to "catch." Or the receptors may be oversensitive, catching more neurotransmitters than they should.

DID YOU KNOW?

About half of people with bipolar disorder develop the illness prior to age 25, and for that group, most often in the teenage years. But it can happen to people much younger and much older.

Who Becomes Bipolar?

Doctors are not completely sure why some people develop bipolar disorders and others do not. Family history probably plays a role. That is, people who have relatives with bipolar disorder may be more likely to have it themselves. But it doesn't happen that way every time. In fact, bipolar disorders can happen to anyone—people of different races, genders, ages, and social classes all can have these problems. Kids as young as five can have bipolar disorder. Sometimes this is called "early **onset**" or "pediatric"

We don't know why some people develop bipolar disorder and others do not. However, researchers believe that, like many other mental problems, bipolar disorder can sometimes run in families.

BIPOLAR DISORDER AND FAMILY HISTORY

If one parent has bipolar disorder, there is a 10 to 30 percent chance that his or her child will develop it, and that number increases if both parents have bipolar disorder. So it is *somewhat* more likely, but it is certainly not definite. Many children with a bipolar parent do not develop bipolar disorder themselves.

bipolar disorder. This type tends to be more severe than in older people.

In the next chapters, we'll talk about how doctors identify bipolar disorders and how the disorders are treated.

Text-Dependent Questions

1. How does the brain send messages?
2. What is a neurotransmitter?
3. What may be happening in the brain of someone who is depressed?

Research Project

Research the different parts of the brain (such as the cortex and the hippocampus) and find out what each part does. Focus on one part and research how injuries to it or problems with it may result in specific mental disorders?

CHAPTER THREE

DIAGNOSING BIPOLAR DISORDERS

Words to Understand

diagnose: to identify a problem.

misdiagnose: to incorrectly identify a problem.

psychiatrist: a medical doctor who specializes in mental disorders.

referral: a recommendation by a doctor to see another doctor or to have additional tests.

Only a mental health professional can say for sure whether someone has bipolar disorder. A family doctor or pediatrician is a good place to start. The doctor will probably run some tests first. This is done to rule out any physical illnesses that could be causing the trouble.

Depending on the test results, the doctor may refer the patient to someone who specializes in mood disorders.

First Appointment

What can you expect from a first appointment with a **psychiatrist** or other mental health professional? During your first visit, you should expect to:

It is okay to bring a trusted adult with you to an appointment with a psychiatrist or counselor. But it is also okay to ask for privacy.

THE TEST MYTH

Years ago, there was a rumor that a bipolar test had been invented. Supposedly this test would make it possible to know right away if someone had a bipolar disorder. But this is completely untrue. There is no magic test to determine if something is wrong. Bipolar disorder is very complicated, and it can take time to figure out.

- be allowed to have a family member along if you want
- spend at least an hour at the appointment
- meet with the doctor and discuss symptoms
- answer detailed questions about medical history
- have the opportunity to ask questions
- be given a **referral** for additional medical tests
- be given a referral for counseling
- possibly be put on psychiatric medication
- be scheduled for follow-up visits
- be free to see a second doctor (This is called "getting a second opinion.")
- be treated with respect

Bipolar Disorders and Other Mental Health Issues

Bipolar disorder can be tricky to **diagnose** for a few reasons. For one thing, people in a manic state often don't believe that they have a problem. They argue that they are "just happy." And because happiness can look different in different people, sometimes it's difficult to tell who is right.

Depressive states can also be tricky. Having "the blues" from time to time is just a part of life, especially for teenagers.

Kids and teens often have different symptoms than adults. It's important to make sure you are seeing the right doctor for you.

At what point do the blues stop being "normal" and start being a problem? The line is not always clear.

Also, a number of other mental health issues can look similar to bipolar disorder. Depression is the most obvious example. What's the difference between someone with bipolar disorder who is having a depressive episode and someone who simply has depression? The difference, of course, is that the person with bipolar disorder will become manic or hypomanic at some point. But that might only become clear over time. It may not be obvious in the first doctor's appointment.

Attention-Deficit Hyperactivity Disorder

One of the most commonly diagnosed disorders among kids is attention-deficit hyperactivity disorder (ADHD). Kids with

ADHD have trouble paying attention for long periods of time. Because of this, sometimes they don't want to even try activities that many other kids like. To them, it doesn't seem worth the effort. Kids with ADHD can be very forgetful and distracted, and they often don't listen when someone speaks to them. They also have trouble sitting still. They tend to talk too much and have trouble waiting their turn. They often wander around a lot, starting activities they can't finish.

Does anything sound familiar about these symptoms? Someone who is distracted and forgetful? Someone who doesn't seem interested in activities that others enjoy? Does this person have ADHD or is she depressed? What about someone who can't sit still and

DID YOU KNOW?

There are about 3.4 million kids in the United States who have depression. Some experts think that as many as one third of these kids may in fact have the early stages of a bipolar disorder.

ADHD VERSUS BIPOLAR: EXAMPLES

The actions of people with bipolar disorder might look similar to those with ADHD on the outside. But things feel very different on the inside.

For instance, it's pretty common for people with ADHD to break things. They don't mean to—they do it by accident, usually because they weren't paying attention. People with bipolar disorder sometimes break things, too. But they usually do it on purpose, in fits of anger.

People with bipolar disorder can be very up or very down, but they can also have periods in the middle, where they seem more "like themselves." People with ADHD do not have these roller-coaster moods. And their disorder does not seem to "go away" for certain periods.

keeps interrupting others? Does this person have ADHD or is she having a manic episode?

The truth is, the behaviors of people with ADHD and those with bipolar disorder can look very similar. But the *cause* of the behaviors is different. People with a bipolar disorder have trouble controlling their moods: They feel *too* happy, *too* angry, *too* sad. People with ADHD might get frustrated sometimes, and they might have trouble controlling their emotions. But in general, they aren't happier or sadder than anyone else.

But because of the similar behaviors, it is fairly common for kids with bipolar disorder to be **misdiagnosed** as having ADHD. Unfortunately, it's also possible for kids to have *both* ADHD and bipolar disorder at the same time, but they are still two different disorders.

Oppositional Defiant Disorder

Oppositional defiant disorder (ODD) is a mental disorder that involves extreme hostility to authority. People with ODD tend to be very irritable and they lose their temper very easily. They provoke arguments with people who have power over them. ODD is mostly diagnosed in kids, but it can continue into adulthood.

It is easy for kids with bipolar disorder to be misdiagnosed with ODD. After all, kids with bipolar disorder can also be both irritable and confrontational when they are in a manic episode. But, at the same time, it is also common for kids with ODD to also have bipolar disorder.

One study found that nearly half of kids with ODD were also suffering from bipolar disorder.

Disruptive Mood Dysregulation Disorder

The name of this disorder may be complicated, but actually, it is pretty straightforward. The prefix *dys-* means "bad" or "ill." So *dysregulation* just means bad regulation—in this case, the inability to control bad feelings. Disruptive mood dysregulation disorder (DMDD) involves extreme irritability and aggressiveness. Kids with DMDD have "rages" or temper tantrums at least three times per week. Symptoms have to last for a year before a doctor will diagnose DMDD.

The behavior of someone with DMDD and someone in a manic episode can seem similar. So it is not uncommon for bipolar disorder and DMDD to be confused. In fact, some experts believe that bipolar might be diagnosed too often. Some of the kids whom we call "bipolar" might really have DMDD. But DMDD is a pretty recent term, so experts will have to study children with these symptoms to learn how to distinguish DMDD from other disorders.

FIND OUT MORE

For more information on ADHD, ODD, and DMDD, check out two other books in this set: *Attention-Deficit Hyperactivity Disorder* and *Disruptive Behavior Disorders*.

Text-Dependent Questions

1. What can you expect from a first appointment with a psychiatrist or other mental health specialist?
2. Why is bipolar disorder so difficult to diagnose?
3. Name some other mental health issues that can be confused with bipolar disorder. Why does this confusion happen?

Research Project

Find out more about mental health services for kids. What are some of the services in your area, and what kinds of programs do they offer? How can these services help kids who are struggling? You might begin your search at the website of the National Association for Mental Illness (www.nami.org), an organization with chapters in all 50 states, plus Washington, DC, Puerto Rico, and the Virgin Islands.

CHAPTER FOUR

LIVING WITH BIPOLAR DISORDER

Words to Understand

anticonvulsant: a medicine given to people who have seizures, but also used for other purposes.

cognitive: having to do with the mind and thought.

compound: a combination of two or more substances.

mood stabilizer: a medicine that helps reduce the extreme highs and lows of someone's emotions.

tolerate: accept.

Bipolar disorder is not a simple problem, and the solutions are not simple, either. A doctor will work with a bipolar patient to create a "treatment plan." For bipolar disorders, treatment plans will probably include both medicine and therapy, plus other lifestyle changes in diet and sleep. Kids with bipolar disorder can usually get extra help with school as well.

Medication

As we discussed in chapter two, bipolar disorder is mainly a problem with brain chemistry. So it makes sense that medicines are used to treat it. Although there is no cure for bipolar disorder, a number of drugs can help people feel better.

Taking medication for a mood disorder is not as simple as taking medication for a headache. You may need to try a few different types or dosages until you find the one that works best.

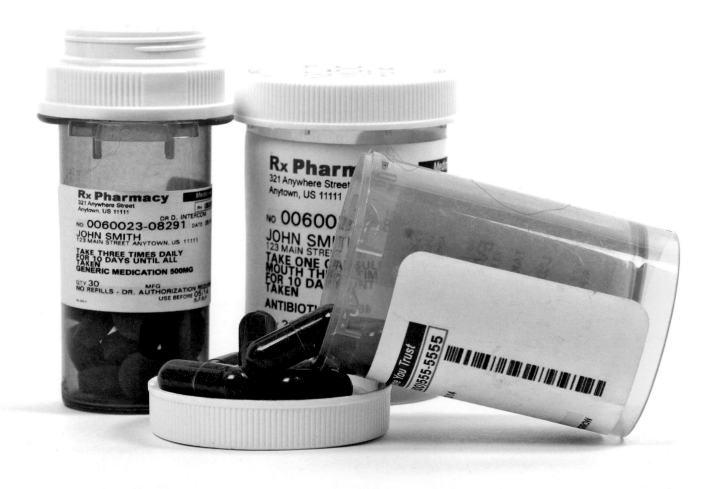

For people with bipolar disorder, the most important drugs are called **mood stabilizers**. These drugs affect neurotransmitters in the brain. They make mood swings less severe. There are a number of types.

Lithium. The first mood stabilizer was lithium, and it is still used today. Lithium has an interesting history. It is actually an element occurring in nature and in the human body. Lithium is used to make certain types of glass, fireworks, and batteries.

Lithium **compounds** were first used as medicine in the 1800s, when doctors prescribed them to treat a kidney disease called gout. Before long, lithium was used for other problems, including manic episodes. But it was not until the 1970s that lithium became a common treatment for bipolar disorder.

Salar de Atacama is a massive, dried-up lake bed in Chile. It is also one of the world's largest sources of lithium.

IF YOU HAVE BIPOLAR DISORDER . . .

If you are starting treatment, there are a few things you should remember:

- *Go easy on yourself.* You will have good days and bad days. That's okay.
- *Try to be patient.* Overcoming a mood disorder takes time.
- *Try to be flexible.* If one treatment option doesn't work, your doctor will suggest you try another.
- *Accept help.* The support of friends and family is essential to success.

Lithium can be very helpful for people with bipolar disorder. However, it also comes with many side effects. Kid's bodies, especially, don't always **tolerate** lithium well. So other mood stabilizers are also used.

Anticonvulsants. These drugs were originally made to help people who have seizures. But, as often happens in medicine, doctors realized that they could also treat other problems. There are a number of different anticonvulsants, and they all work a bit differently. Some are better at some things than others.

In the 1990s, a new type of medication was developed called atypical antipsychotics. These drugs help people who are having trouble organizing their thoughts. They are also calming for people who have problems controlling their moods, and they can help kids who are aggressive and have temper outbursts. They are often prescribed in combination with other medicines.

This brings us to an important fact about treating bipolar disorder. Because the disorder involves several different moods, people are often treated with several different medicines. There are many available, and they all affect different people in slightly different ways. And all these drugs have side effects. Some side effects are easy to tolerate, but some aren't. If you (or someone you know) is being treated for bipolar disorder, it is important to keep the doctor aware of whatever side effects may occur.

A doctor may have to try a number of different drug combinations. It can take as long as a year for someone with bipolar disorder to find the right medicines at the right doses. It's difficult to be patient when you or someone you love is suffering. But it's important to remember that a doctor is not a magician. It may take time, but eventually your doctor can help figure out what works best.

PARTS OF A TREATMENT PLAN

Treatment plans for bipolar disorder vary from person to person. But there are some common elements, including:

- medication
- monitoring (that is, paying close attention to moods, behavior, and side effects of drugs)
- therapy for both the person and his or her family
- extra help or special programs at school
- learning about the illness
- sticking to healthy diet
- getting regular exercise
- getting regular sleep

Adapted from "About Pediatric Bipolar Disorder," http://www.thebalanced mind.org/learn/library/about-pediatric-bipolar-disorder?page=all, March 24, 2014.

Therapy

In addition to medicine, most people with bipolar disorder have some type of therapy as well. This can involve "talk therapy" like you might have seen on TV, where someone sits in a doctor's office and discusses his feelings and behavior. But for bipolar disorder, **cognitive**-behavioral therapy (CBT) might be even more helpful.

CBT has two parts. The cognitive part involves teaching the person to think differently about his disorder. For example, people with bipolar disorder learn that their extreme feelings are symptoms, not "true" feelings. This can help them feel more in control of their mood swings.

The second aspect of CBT relates to behavior. The person learns to act in ways that are more healthy or positive. People with bipolar disorder can learn habits that will help stabilize their moods. One very simple example is sleep: Getting good, regular sleep is an important part of managing bipolar disorder. Or, someone with bipolar disorder might learn steps to take when he feels a manic episode is about to start.

Mood Charts

Because bipolar disorder involves extreme changes in mood, it makes sense to keep track of these feelings. On a mood chart, a person records how she felt that day (usually on a scale from "extremely depressed" to "extremely manic"). The chart also asks what medication the person is taking, and when; how much the person slept; if she exercised; and what she ate.

Many therapists use mood charts to help people study their mood swings over time. For example, a person might learn

Day of Month	1	2	3	4	5	6
Make a checkmark in the box that matches your symptoms for that day. *If you felt more than one way at different times, check more than one box.*						
Extremely Manic						
Very Manic						
Somewhat Manic						
Mildly Manic						
Stable						
Mildly Depressed						
Somewhat Depressed						
Very Depressed						
Extremely Depressed						
Mixed						
Medication *(Make a checkmark if medication was taken that day.)*						
Medication						
Sleep						
Total Hours Slept						
Uninterrupted Sleep						
Food						
Number of Meals						
Number of Snacks						

Mood charting can be done on paper. The user fills in the boxes with information every day. There are also apps that make it possible to chart moods using cell phones and tablets.

that she is more likely to feel "down" on days when she didn't sleep well the night before. Mood charts can also be useful in tracking whether or not a particular medicine is working.

Final Thought: Having versus Being

You might have heard someone say, "so-and-so is bipolar." But this is not accurate. A person is not bipolar disorder; a person *has* bipolar disorder. This might seem like a tiny difference, but it isn't tiny at all.

Think about the last time you had a cold. Did you become a different person? No, of course not. You were still you, just with a runny nose. Mental disorders are really no different. People who have bipolar disorder are still themselves. Their symptoms are just that: symptoms of an illness. It can help to picture these disorders as something separate from ourselves. The disorder isn't you, but it is something you carry along with you.

Bipolar disorder is not an easy illness to carry. But with a good doctor, a good treatment plan, and the support of family and friends, people with bipolar disorder can have terrific lives.

IF SOMEONE YOU KNOW HAS BIPOLAR DISORDER . . .

Here are some tips for helping someone with bipolar disorder:

- *Learn about the illness.* The more you know about the disorder, the easier it will be to cope.
- *Be a good listener.* Pay attention to what the person is saying and what he or she needs.
- *Make plans.* Accept that bad days will happen sometimes. When the person is calm, make plans for what you should do when he or she is having an episode.
- *Support treatment.* Try to help the person stay positive about treatment and stay on schedule with medications.
- *Look after yourself, too.* It's stressful to be a good friend to someone with bipolar disorder. Make sure that you are taking care of yourself as well.

If you are concerned that someone you know is thinking about hurting himself or herself, talk to a trusted adult. This is not something kids should have to handle without help.

Text-Dependent Questions

1. What is a treatment plan? What are some things that are almost always included in treatment plans?
2. What is the main type of medicine used to treat bipolar disorders? What does it do?
3. What is CBT, and what does it do?

Research Project

Make your own mood chart. You can download paper copies from the Internet or copy the one given in the chapter. Fill out the chart every day for at least a week. The longer you stick with it, the more you will learn. What do you see about your moods over time? Do sleep, food, and exercise have any impact on how you feel?

Further Reading

BOOKS

Jamieson, Patrick E. *Mind Race: A First-Hand Account of One Teenager's Experience with Bipolar Disorder.* New York: Oxford University Press, 2006.

Kiesbye, Stefan. *Bipolar Disorder*. Farmington Hills, MI: Greenhaven, 2010.

Miklowitz, David J., and Elizabeth L. George. *The Bipolar Teen: What You Can Do to Help Your Child and Your Family.* New York: Guildford Press, 2008.

Papolos, Demitri, and Janice Papolos. *The Bipolar Child: The Definitive and Reassuring Guide to Childhood's Most Misunderstood Disorder.* 3rd ed. New York: Broadway Books, 2006.

ONLINE

The Balanced Mind Parent Network. http://www.thebalancedmind.org.

KidsHealth. "Bipolar Disorder."

http://kidshealth.org/kid/health_problems/learning_problem/bipolar_disorder.html.

National Institute of Mental Health. "Bipolar Disorder in Children and Teens."

http://www.nimh.nih.gov/health/publications/bipolar-disorder-in-children-and-teens-easy-to-read/index.shtml.

LOSING HOPE?

This free, confidential phone number will connect you to counselors who can help.

National Suicide Prevention Lifeline

1-800-273-TALK (1-800-273-8255)

"Mental illness is nothing to be ashamed of, but stigma and bias shame us all. Together, we will replace stigma with acceptance, ignorance with understanding, fear with new hope for the future. Together, we will build a stronger nation for the new century, leaving no one behind."
—Bill Clinton

Series Glossary

acute: happening powerfully for a short period of time.

affect: as a noun, the way someone seems on the outside—including attitude, emotion, and voice (pronounced with the emphasis on the first syllable, "AFF-eckt").

atypical: different from what is usually expected.

bipolar: involving two, opposite ends.

chronic: happening again and again over a long period of time.

comorbidity: two or more illnesses appearing at the same time.

correlation: a relationship or connection.

delusion: a false belief with no connection to reality.

dementia: a mental disorder, featuring severe memory loss.

denial: refusal to admit that there is a problem.

depressant: a substance that slows down bodily functions.

depression: a feeling of hopelessness and lack of energy.

deprivation: a hurtful lack of something important.

diagnose: to identify a problem.

empathy: understanding someone else's situation and feelings.

epidemic: a widespread illness.

euphoria: a feeling of extreme, even overwhelming, happiness.

hallucination: something a person sees or hears that is not really there.

heredity: the passing of a trait from parents to children.

hormone: a substance in the body that helps it function properly.

hypnotic: a type of drug that causes sleep.

impulsivity: the tendency to act without thinking.

inattention: distraction; not paying attention.

insomnia: inability to fall asleep and/or stay asleep.

licensed: having an official document proving one is capable with a certain set of skills.

manic: a high level of excitement or energy.

misdiagnose: to incorrectly identify a problem.

moderation: limited in amount, not extreme.

noncompliance: refusing to follow rules or do as instructed.

onset: the beginning of something; pronounced like "on" and "set."

outpatient: medical care that happens while a patient continues to live at home.

overdiagnose: to determine more people have a certain illness than actually do.

pediatricians: doctors who treat children and young adults.

perception: awareness or understanding of reality.

practitioner: a person who actively participates in a particular field.

predisposition: to be more likely to do something, either due to your personality or biology.

psychiatric: having to do with mental illness.

psychiatrist: a medical doctor who specializes in mental disorders.

psychoactive: something that has an effect on the mind and behavior.

psychosis: a severe mental disorder where the person loses touch with reality.

psychosocial: the interaction between someone's thoughts and the outside world of relationships.

psychotherapy: treatment for mental disorders.

relapse: getting worse after a period of getting better.

spectrum: a range; in medicine, from less extreme to more extreme.

stereotype: a simplified idea about a type of person, not connected to actual individuals.

stimulant: a substance that speeds up bodily functions.

therapy: treatment of a problem; can be done with medicine or simply by talking with a therapist.

trigger: something that causes something else.

Index

Page numbers in *italics* refer to photographs.

About the Author

H. W. POOLE is a writer and editor of books for young people, such as the *Horrors of History* series (Charlesbridge). She is also responsible for many critically acclaimed reference books, including *Political Handbook of the World* (CQ Press) and the *Encyclopedia of Terrorism* (SAGE). She was coauthor and editor of the *History of the Internet* (ABC-CLIO), which won the 2000 American Library Association RUSA award.

About the Advisor

ANNE S. WALTERS is Clinical Associate Professor of Psychiatry and Human Behavior. She is the Clinical Director of the Children's Partial Hospital Program at Bradley Hospital, a program that provides partial hospital level of care for children ages 7–12 and their families. She also serves as Chief Psychologist for Bradley Hospital. She is actively involved in teaching activities within the Clinical Psychology Training Programs of the Alpert Medical School of Brown University and serves as Child Track Seminar Co-Coordinator. Dr. Walters completed her undergraduate work at Duke University, graduate school at Georgia State University, internship at UTexas Health Science Center, and postdoctoral fellowship at Brown University. Her interests lie in the area of program development, treatment of severe psychiatric disorders in children, and psychotic spectrum disorders.

Photo Credits

Photos are for illustrative purposes only; individuals depicted in the photos, both on the cover and throughout this book, are only models.

Cover Photo: iStock.com/CraigRJD

Dollar Photo Club: 10 Roman Milert; 12 bramgino; 13 alma05; 14 Ilike; 21 CGinspiration; 23 imtmphoto; 26 Lisa F. Young; 31 stefanolunardi; 35 Rob Byron; 36 Arun; 41 Radosław Brzozo. **iStock.com:** 20 Orchidpoet; 28 Clark and Company. **Library of Congress:** 16.